EARTHEN JAR

EARTHEN JAR

*Enjoy my earthen jar,
stuffed full of experiences.*

Fondly,

Raynette

Raynette Eitel

To order additional copies of this book, contact:
Xlibris Corporation
1-888-795-4274
www.Xlibris.com
Orders@Xlibris.com
45948

CONTENTS

DEDICATION

This book is dedicated to my husband, Jim, who has been open to sharing my life as a poet and my three daughters, Risa Biggar, Shaunna Howat, and Krissa Ferguson, who lived in the middle of many of these poems.

PREFACE

Earthen Jar is a vessel of poetry written over the years of my lifetime. May the metaphors within this book be rain upon your fallow ground and may they bring a new spring growth deep within your being.

Raynette Eitel

EARTHEN JAR

I am an earthen jar
saturated with memories
to pour upon the scorched earth
during drought.

FLY-AWAY POEMS

Poems come to me at night
when I am drugged with sleep
and hardly hear their whispers.
Offended, they fly away like bats
to sleep by day in caves.
They hang there upside down,
dreaming, perhaps, of
my tossing and turning,
my trying to piece together
snatches of a poem
that flew away.

APPLE DREAM

It is time to pick dreams like apples,
peeling them back
to make thin, white slices
ready to eat.

Dust the sour ones with sugar
mounded like snow.
On the dried and shriveled,
pour a bit of sweet wine.

Then should I hear God speak
from out of the heavens,
I shall hide beneath my pillow
and blame you for making
me pick the apple.

BEAR DANCING

It is White Night in St. Petersburg and
a brown bear dances beside the Neva
to the sounds of a wheezing accordion
and cameras clicking like busy sparrows.

His clumsy form is so farcical,
menace disguised like a KGB spy,
eyes shielding wildness born deep in the forest
where secrets are kept and spirits run free.

Now the captive, he performs
a sadly maniacal dark dance,
swaying to the grief he locks away
in his heart as we applaud and cheer.

It is White Night in St. Petersburg
and we take home tatters of memory
of a shattered old bear dancing his pain
as a midnight sun paints his anguished face.

FLOWERS FROM A WEDDING

After the wedding, her parents
took bouquets to a nursing home
where patients clapped their hands,
remembering weddings and music and love.

That night the men reveled in
wonderful wet, salty dreams
and awakened with satisfied smiles.

The women dreamed Godiva dreams
of riding white horses through spring meadows
with garlands of forget-me-nots
across their beautiful, perky breasts.
Come morning they were blessed
with a dewy radiance and fragrance of flowers.

All that day coquettish smiles swept through
a bouquet-laden social room, as well as
some shy hand-holding between wheel chairs.
Nurses found the patients easier to put to bed
as the old folks looked forward to dreaming again.

The flowers wilted in a day or so,
along with the lust.

CELEBRATIONS

Didn't we know how to celebrate
when we blew new balloons,
hanging them like fruit on the old tree
in the front yard.

Didn't we know how to celebrate
with bottles of full-bodied wine
and golden wheels of cheese
we brought from the cellar.
We touched our glasses,
sang out, "Salud!"
then drank, feeling the liquid
warm our tongues and hearts.

Didn't we know how to celebrate
as the fiddle took up the cause
and you whirled me in your arms
beneath sweet, swirling moonlight.
Fireworks competing with stars
scattered across the heavens
with a mighty bang,
leaving us breathless
with joy.

Didn't we know how to celebrate.
with birthday cake, candles,
wishes, kisses, and dreams shared
for all the yesterdays and tomorrows
left to celebrate our love,
pasting memories in the scrapbook
of our minds.

FOG HOLDS LIGHTS

Fog holds lights in soft hands stroking
the bay, floating across waters alive
with flickering rays. The night air whispers

of ancient sand castles and the gleam
of small stars stirring the romance of darkness.
It clings faithfully to the rise and fall

of waves washing in, swinging to
the rhythm of a sea singing love songs.
Fog holds lights in soft hands, clasps love

in tender touches, grasps hope in strong
fingers as it rolls in. Reality
blurs, an impressionist painting

lying just under the murky paint of fog.
Fog holds light in soft hands, embraces
dreams carefully as they swoop

across our sleep like moonbeams prowling
the night sky. It smothers the future and remolds
the past, leaving us in a blurred limbo.

Fog holds light in soft hands wet with tears.
When it is time for it to be gone,
it lifts silently and disappears.

OLD POET

I have reached the age
where my feet move slowly enough
for words to catch up,
skipping along in iambic pentameter.

Once I hopped over merry metaphors
rolling like marbles in front of me
so I would not fail to notice.

There was a time when rhyme
rang in my ears like a lullaby,
when alliteration clung to my tongue
like licking lime lollipops
until my lips puckered.

Now, weary words wander blithely
across my pages,
recalling passion, laughter, tears
from other years
then leaving a sort of peace.

I don't mind that my life
is in the final couplet of a sonnet.
The first twelve lines were superb.
I expect only that the ending rhyme
will in all due time
be unique and pleasing to the ear.

YOUNG GIRL'S AUDITION

Flute held in hands
trying not to tremble,
lips taut, breath controlled,
Mozart brushing the keys lightly,
Bach's notes falling quick as rain,
art from the very soul
of a young girl who knows
her future depends on this.

She holds herself straight, proud,
fingering keys with agility,
whistle tones surprising even herself,
a virtuoso in the making,
vibrato blooming like spring flowers.

Judges watch, listen,
nod and smile
at youth dancing within
another century,
tripping lightly over grace notes
meant to dazzle the senses
and sweetness delighting the soul.

When the music stops,
there is this realization
they were holding their breath
as this silver flute became the magic
from times of old.

DREAMS IN THE WIND

Your dreams quiver in the wind,
whisk themselves across your face
and out of sight. Your hand trembles
as you pen the last memory
of a cherished dream gone missing.

Words you write do not tell
the whole story. You send hope
like a test balloon, checking
the strength of the wind. Each word
scatters like bubbles, bright rainbows
shivering across a cold sky.

Still you write, jaw set,
pen in a determined fist
capturing images of dreams
lingering in long shadows,
hiding in musty book shelves,
photo albums, piano keys,
love letters . . . each waiting
for you to discover them.

There's no time for despair,
anger, weeping, just this prayer
that getting the images in place
will bring love to every heart
and hope enough to grasp like a rope
tossed out for salvation.

The dream blew away, but now
you become the hope, the love
that refused to be lost.
Your words no longer wander, lost
in the wilderness of dreams
for you have brought them home to stay.

ALL THESE YEARS AFTER THE FUNERAL

All these years after the funeral,
casseroles still taste like death.
Salted with tears,
layered with mournful noodles,
every bite is bitter with grief.

It isn't that I didn't appreciate
those acts of love
brought in hot and steaming,
bubbling with cheery cheese,
bright vegetables chopped like confetti
and ready to feed the children.

It isn't that I meant to be rude
to good friends trying to help;
but I was an alien in my own kitchen
learning to decipher the recipe for sorrow,
attempting to elude panic simmering in my heart
while casseroles, cakes, and shivering Jello salads
gathered on the table like disease.

All these years after the funeral
my heartbreak has nearly healed
but my taste buds are damaged forever.

DEJA VU

In one century or another, I lived behind
these dark-green shuttered windows
with bougainvillea reaching to the roof.
This farmhouse was once lighted
by lanterns and laughter and love.
My family lived within these walls.
(I miss them still.)

In spring I walked these dusty roads of Tuscany,
climbing through the hill country,
pausing to rest beneath an ancient olive tree.
I watched sunlight wash across sienna stonework
of the tall bell tower,
content with the image of Mama at home,
stirring soup for the evening meal.
(I smell that soup today.)

One summer day I stopped beside that wall
to sit in the shade with a friend.
She dipped cool water
from her family's well.
We gossiped gently for a time,
our soft words lyrical as an opera.
(I no longer remember Italian.)

In autumn harvest I picked our vineyard's grapes,
rolling the sweet, soft marbles of fruit
over my tongue until at last the juice spurted
into my greedy mouth.
I tasted the first of the Chianti.
(I taste it still.)

One winter I entered this Romanesque church,
lit a candle, warming my hands, my heart, my soul.
I knelt to pray at the altar, shivering from the cold.
The priest's rhythmic footsteps on the tile floor
echo even now in my dreams.
(When I find the stone marking my grave,
I will leave a flower.)

HORSE DREAMS

When the handicappers
rein in the figures in preparation
for the race,

When they stand in queues,
cash in hand, quivering to watch
the unknown,

When the last bet is in place,
starting gate loaded,
breath held,

It becomes at last obvious
they didn't think about
a grand vision

Of a small, determined jockey
or the sweet dreams a dark horse had
of crossing a finish line first.

AFTER THE KNIFE

. . . and for the rest of her life,
that unwanted child came to her in dreams
walking without a sound on wounded feet.
There had been no rain
For forty days and forty nights
And the ground was hot.

She waited for her, wondering what to say
To this child with wounded feet and a bruised heart
as she stepped through dreams beneath ruthless stars
threatening to fall.

She waited for the child who kept walking
In silence, growing smaller as she came closer
Until at last she disappeared, leaving
Bloody footprints across the sands of dreams.

HOW TO CRITIQUE A POEM

Go slowly.
Nibble it around the edges and sigh.
Lick the sugar off the top
then close your eyes, remembering
Christmas and Mom's oven candy stores
with cases of jeweled jelly beans.

Write it down.

Now fondle it line by line,
feeling its depth and breadth,
its smooth, seamless surface,
its throbbing core,
its beating heart.

Describe it.

Walk its path.
Bury your nose in its scent.
Search out tangled weeds,
bees inside a rose.
Check for stumbling stones,
watch for wolves wandering the darkness,
Count the dangers one by one.

Make a list.

Cram the poem into your heart.
Hear the beat of its music.
Be aware of hidden silver tears,
embrace the indigo sadness,
unwrap the lilac lilt of laughter,
tap the black night of anger,
unbridled white emotion,
harnessed red energy,
grey granite grief, golden love.
Decipher the formula.

Now give the poet his due.

JAZZ TEARS

Jazz stirred in a cold martini,
staccato beating frozen memories
upon my fragile struggling heart.

Sounds of jazz are twins to twilight,
A soft soothing of indigo grief
great waves crashing over my body.

Warm jazz tears wash down my cheeks
in salty streaks of silver sadness.
Sweet images of the past

done in syncopated notes,
soft and mellow as golden moonlight,
call my ghosts to dance again.

Jazz tears and old fears hum,
blends of sadness and euphoria.
My martini twirls in the glass.

LAZARUS

I am Lazarus in the tomb,
Cold and covered by darkness,
Awaiting a certain voice.

31

FAITH

You see, faith is the thing
So it doesn't matter
Who derides you,
Who places a crown of thorns
On your head
Or hands you a cross to carry.

When you know
Someone turned water into wine,
And you are sure
Stones can be rolled away
From caves where the dead sleep
And One who was put there didn't stay,

You don't need to see it.
You have that peace
Coming from understanding
That holding evidence in your hand
And storing evidence in your heart
Are not equal.
In order to believe it.

You know it is true
The same way you know
A rainbow will
Fill the sky after a rain
To make certain you remember about faith.

FINGERTIPS

Fingertips on my forehead,
a prelude played pizzicato
with my heartstrings.

STEPPING STONES TO SHAKESPEARE

When you were a child,
I offered stepping stones to Shakespeare,
Handing you delicious words, like mints,
To melt upon your tongue.
The language did not take us
Straight to castles of the Bard
But along quiet paths
Twisting around enchanted forests
Through thick and leafy phrases.

You wore pajamas and smelled of innocence.
I held you close as ghosts
Whispered shadowy secrets.
We strolled straight through
A looking glass together,
Collecting magic moments
Like small white doves
We might one day pull from a hat
And watch as they fly away.

Oh my dear, the lands we saw
And the characters we met
Gave us stories like soft silk scarves
To slip from our sleeves when needed.
Each night we traveled our well-worn path
With laughter or terror or sadness until
Your eyes became heavy with sleep.

I took your small, sweet hand
Leading you straight
To your safe sailboat of a bed.
Kissing you softly, I sent you off
To embark on a midsummer night's dream
Of *"flights of angels singing you to your rest."**

**Hamlet, Vii*

EARTHQUAKE

The day the earth moved in Columbia,
The day the two hundred year old church
Crashed down on the cross,
Leaving Jesus lying in the rubble,
Juan Paco Ruiz ran for his life.

He ran like a peg-legged pirate
While the earth pitched,
While the ground rolled like the ocean
And tall masts of trees trembled,
Tumbling from their places.

Stark terror took hold of his feet,
His heart, his brain.
He passed toppled walls,
Ominous in their silence.
He ran by crowds of sobbing women
And children too dazed to cry.

He changed course when he saw
Great stone chunks of the church
Strewn across the cluttered street,
Stone slabs scattered
Like so many grave markers.
So many.

He recalled his ordinary morning
Saying goodbye
To his wife and mother
As they left for mass.
Now they must be lying here
Buried with God.
Buried by God.
Muerte con Cristo.
Run! Run!

Juan Paco gasped for air,
Blinded to the chaos around him.
He could not say why he was running.
He knew only that his innocent family
And his blameless village,
Like Sodom and Gomorrah, were destroyed;
And that, remembering Lot's unfortunate wife,
He mustn't look back.

LOVE AND ANGUISH

Love and anguish languish here,
Siamese twins of a life
lived to the fullest.

Let love in the door
but accept anguish
lingering with sighs of pain
and eyes cast down in shame.

Allow anguish to enter,
and you will be lucky enough
to have love slip silently into
your heart and soul
bringing soft comfort and warm healing
tied by the sturdy rope of hope to grab
when you may be drowning.

Love and anguish languish here
soaked with tears of joy and grief,
woven with threads of a life's pages,
singing your song and
whispering words across the ages.

CHERRY BLOSSOMS

In the Tidal Basin,
Cherry trees hold blossoms
As an offering to spring.

Tourists flock like birds,
Chirping their pictures
Gathering photo ops
Like so many seeds.

There is too much talking
On this holy ground.
One should be able
To sit quietly
Inhaling beauty with fragrance.

A small Japanese girl
Stands beneath a tree
Becoming one with beauty
With nature
With history.

MELANOMA BUTTERFLY

I lie beside you while this butterfly stain
between your shoulders
shudders and undulates
its colored wings.

I watch this metamorphosis,
this fluttering *dance macabre*,
as wings grow large, small,
blue, then red,
shrieking their neon message
only to me.
You do not see it.

I, who loved to kiss your skin,
and taste the salty strength of you
now taste only my own tears
while your butterfly flutters
deep beneath your skin
as though returning
to a cocoon.

AT OCTOBERFEST

When they played the "Beer Barrel Polka,"
when the dancers moved their feet faster
than a Bavarian baritone could play,
music bounced across the worn floor
in grains of joy like rice strewn at weddings,
like gaggles of giggles from small children.
Confettied sounds of happiness rained down
like rainbowed drops of mirth in song.

The whirling dancers, the twirling, couples
tripped lightly on top of bright ribbons of notes,
exuding gaiety as the polka
made its never-ending promise of pleasure.
Every thought of sadness was strained out
in a grid of grace notes and the oompah
of a bright Octoberfest beneath
a shiny gold beer-barrel moon.

I COME TO THE SEA

I come to the sea
to hear clear whispers
of old dreams.

While an ancient moon hums
snatches of golden melodies
over bass clefs of waves,
I listen as forgotten voices
sing soothing songs across the water.
Salt stings my cheeks.

I come to the sea
for the sound of surf slipping
secrets into my sleep,
loosening grief long calcified
and washing it away on the tide.

Come morning,
I shall hear confetti sounds
of celebration laced with bird calls,
children's lyrical laughter,
and lines of flapping, colorful kites
riding the humming wind.
Then I shall rise to walk the beach
in peace.

FLUTE GAME

A flute sounds above the sadness I hold,
its sweet breath filled with innocence.
It cavorts playfully, tugs at my sleeves,

clowns in triplets, tucks phrases of notes
inside my blue mood, begs me to join in.
The flute is a young child who cannot know

heartbreak or a wounded, broken spirit.
It is light as gold dust on a sunbeam,
fireflies twisting in a twilight ballet,

a voice of one painting purity of snow angels,
of young lovers watching stars like tears.
It does not try to soothe, but calls in mischief,

bidding me to find my long lost smile.
And then, in a sudden revelation,
the flute pauses as if to hear my heart.

It starts to play a long lament, a minor
key salted with startling, hidden sadness,
a melancholy melody holding

notes soft with sorrow and fervent prayer,
finding its way to add balm to wounds
giving me at last permission to cry.

It is as though it knows, perhaps, that once
tears are unleashed, I am sure to follow
those twittering flute games to ecstasy.

DREAMS OF A HANGING TREE

When a dream dies,
it is as though it were
sent to a hanging tree.

They march it in,
facing a surly crowd.
Younger dreams watch and learn.

The noose goes around,
stool kicked out
and the dream dangles,

kicking at first,
twitching and twisting silently
drawing its last breath

while the onlookers nod
and stare mercilessly
until there's no more movement.

The dreamer wears widow's black.
Her eyes are dry holes like graves,
mourning her loss.

"Dreams die hard," someone murmurs
as they walk away
from the hanging tree.

No one marks a grave.

DRY SPELL

Words have stopped,
Songs silenced,
Paints dried, flaking,
Feet no longer tapping rhythms.

It is a sort of death;
Living, yet without breath,
A rigor mortis of the soul,
This halt in creativity.

Something eclipsed
The silver moon of spontaneity,
The rainbow glow of promise,
Leaving only a cold, shadowy
Place to mourn
A loss.

BAKING

At night, I wake up sweating
And feel poems baking in my heart
Like my grandmother's biscuits.
As I toss and turn, they brown and rise.
I test each one and add a pat of butter here,
Some honey there, a bit of jam.
I will savor them with my morning coffee.

TEABAG

I am a teabag of poetry
used over and over
until I produce a perfect couplet

WORD THREADS

Poems are woven of word threads
bit by bit
little pieces of silk thoughts
becoming flags to fly
from the place of Pain,
the country of Joy,
the lilting land of Laughter.

GOING UNDER THE MUSIC

Going under the music as a mystic
meandering around each delicate sound,
each grace note skipping to an overture like children
at play. It is an adventure to cherish,
a beauty to sustain a rapacious soul.

Going under the music is swimming
beneath a sea of symphony, seeing a universe
with ears rather than eyes. It is gliding
beneath precious chords and canons of history,
mystery wrapping itself like softest silk
around the heart, until there is only harmony.

Going under the music is clothing oneself
in brocade robes woven from sound, patterned by
composers who penned notes in black ink,
yet set their compositions in fullest color.
One wears music like a garment of springtime
or an embroidered cloth of heavy summer air
improbably sewn with bright autumn leaves
as the heart pumps in frost-laden staccato.

Going under the music is being overcome
by the sweet nectar perfume of cellos,
fluid floral fragrance of fine French horns,
innocent violet scent of violins stroked,
gardenia whiff of flutes singing,
pepper of piccolos sprinkling flakes
of notes with flagrant abandon, pungency of drums
overspreading the hot house of a fugue.

Going under the music is speaking the language
of the universe, the utterance of beauty,
sounds of purest love, then finding them good
and memorizing the sounds for a lifetime of bliss.

CHOKING ON RAINBOWS

The day the son of Ana Maria de Santos
was swept from her arms
by a hillside of mud
was the last time she saw colors.
She spent the rest of her life
choking on rainbows,
and cursing God
under gray, weeping skies.

A blinding rage
ravished Ana Maria de Santos,
rolling over her
in thick, scalding lava,
until she became an ancient ruin
desecrated by elements.

A black blanket of dreams
covered her each night,
smothered her in the darkness,
strangled her
as she searched the starless sky
for a sunrise she could not see.

And to this day,
her eyes filled with mud,
ears plugged,
she gags on rainbows
dancing about her face
as she turns away to mourn.

CAROUSEL

On the carousel, I choose the horse
with flowered collar and demons in his eyes,
put there, they whisper, by Lady Godiva.

A drunken, careening ride begins with blasts
of calliope music from old circuses.
I hang on tightly, sorry I am alone,

wishing you were here to whisper courage
in my ears. The horse goes up and down,
round and round to nowhere to somewhere

to the magical place where it first began.
I see an image of you in bits of mirrors
as I go past then lose it way too soon,

like a cruel door slamming in my face,
like dropping the gold ring and knowing it
it may never delight my eager hands again.

Oh my dear, this wild ride doesn't last
long enough for me to see it all,
feel all there is to feel, or grasp anything

with certainty as my poor head spins.
(But still, there you were in the mirrors
and I nearly captured that golden ring.)

BURY ME WITH CHOCOLATES

Bury me with chocolates,
The kind I love so well.
Send dark and bitter candy wreaths
With leaves of caramel.

Chocolate chip tears upon my cheeks,
White chocolate pillows filled with creams
To soothe me in my final sleep
And sweeten all my heavenly dreams.

Place one lone lovely chocolate rose
With petals curling in my hand.
Heap gold foil coins in random piles,
Egyptian-like, and oh so grand.

Please do not toast me with champagne,
A rich hot chocolate will do,
Laced with a touch of cinnamon
And then perhaps marshmallows too.

But if you plan a conflagration
To send me warmly to my rest,
Do not forget I've always loved
A sticky, hot fudge Sundae best.

BASSOON

There is something so comforting in the sound
of a shiny bassoon singing strongly and deeply,
filling all the dark corners of a concert hall.

Even violins quit whining and hum in tune
with piccolos pecking like sparrows hunting seeds.
Notes from the flutes flutter down like wee petals

leaving a springtime tree. The old bassoon
cups his sounds around fragrant blooms
and holds harmony carefully with aged hands.

When the brass instruments try to intimidate him
his laugh is infectious, leaping smoothly across
the trombone's slide, ignoring blasts from a trumpet

Percussive thunder from ancient kettle drums
Never frightens him. His tone says,
"Be at peace. Taste harmony with love."

Then the audience stops their restless stirring
and hears him with calm hearts and easy ears.
At last, the maestro takes his final bows.

There is something so comforting in the sound
of a shiny bassoon singing strongly and deeply,
filling all the dark corners of a concert hall.

THE DAY THE PLANES QUIT FLYING

The day the planes quit flying over America,
An empty sky was filled with flames,
With mournful clouds
Weeping shrapnel and ash,
Burying innocence.

The day the planes quit flying over America,
Evil Davids tossed missiles
At twin Goliaths
And the world watched their fall.

The day the planes quit flying over America,
Grief rolled down the streets
In a ball of fire,
In a stream of smoke
Eclipsing the sun.
The day was dark,
The nightmare real.

The day the planes quit flying over America,
We watched the pentagon,
That proud eagle,
Bleeding flames from its open wound.
Then that brave bird raised his head
Ready to fly
Like a phoenix rising from ashes.
He moved swiftly,
Eyes wary, searching,
Finding creatures hiding under rocks.

The day the planes quit flying over America,
Goodness began surpassing evil,
Lives laid down for others,
Heroes staring down unmitigated malice,
Flags filling empty spaces,
Candles lighted in dark places,
Love wrapping itself,
Cocoon-like around devastation.

And the world watching had no doubt
That butterflies
Would emerge one day,
The day the planes quit flying over America.

BIRTH DAY

After the heart-stopping, mind-boggling,
bruising day braving the birth canal,
Joey was born.

Too tired to cry, he turned blue and
waited to see what would happen next.

When the doctor swatted his bare bottom,
Joey saw what life was all about and
tried to play dead.
It didn't work. They spanked him again
and blew cold air on his wet stomach.

That did it.
He gave an outraged cry,
fists waving in the air,
and hoped the next birthday
would be better than this.

ACQUIESCENCE

When sleep stays outside
with a demanding moon
and dreams desert me,
leaving only dark images
of days gone by,

when my bed seems like
a cold white prison
and I lie there
listening to something
in the trees,

when my heart skips beats,
leaping like a frog
Inside my chest,
there is no rest.

There is this waiting,
this listening,
this passive acquiescence
of darkness before dawn
and the possibility
that morning may never come . . .
this time.

GROWING OLD

Year by year I feel youth escape
from my pores,
leaving behind this wrinkled flesh
and old songs flaking across my parched lips.

Once I rejoiced in mornings,
breathed in the perfume of dawn,
sipped the elixir of each new day.
Now I wear the veil of twilight casually,
knowing midnight will soon come
and the glass slipper of life
will slide from my foot
and disappear.

While my mirrored image shows age
streaking my face with charcoal lines,
wrinkles like a road map of my life
etch my eyes my mouth my neck.
I search desperately for the girl who
wore gardenias in her hair
as she danced beneath a sky
dusted with dreams and stars.

I glance at my hands,
despondent to discover
they are the arthritic hands of my mother
and my grandmother,
swollen with holding youth too tightly
and stiff from grasping old dreams.

Still the soothing sounds of symphonies
play in the theatre of my soul,
echoes of youth blooming
in the fragrance of flutes,
kettle drums building a child's excitement
in the pit of my stomach
and lullabies sung softly
as I am rocked by loving arms
in the music of memories.

GREEN*

It is the green that covers my dreams
of Lake Windermere's verdant words
left like raindrops by Wordsworth,
streaks of golden daffodils
and stanzas dotted with white sheep
clouds along the lush hills.

I cup the green in my hands,
my heart, my leafy memories
to carry to my desert home
and unfold them on dry, sandy,
sun-baked summer days and smile.

*Ambleside, England

ICARUS KITE

I sent our love, like an Icarus kite
flying into the sunburned sky,
showing off the jeweled colors
to the world, the dazzling symbol
rising higher and ever higher
toward a forbidden sun until
it was only a spinning flame.

At last the kite was black ashes
spinning silently toward earth.
I will recover each precious handful
and scatter them along the shore,
come summer, beneath an osprey flying
alone, seeking something lost.

INNER SIGHT

Your pain comes in waves
entering my body like water,
seeking each crevice
like air filling lungs,
like grains of sand
embedding themselves
within each pore.

It has always been so.
Gypsies have the same gift,
inner sight,
seeing what can't be seen,
knowing what was never known.
They hide their thoughts
in crystal globes,
fingers fluttering,
eyes closed as window shades,
voices shrill with warning.

My gift lacks all that mystery.
I share your pain,
I touch your hand,
never daring read your palm
for fear what I might find.
But I never send you
out of the folds of my tent
to bear it all alone.

MEMORIES HIDING

Memories hide
In caverns of the mind,
Clinging
Like stalactites overhead,
Ringing
With songs of youth,
Tones of the heart.

TATTOOS

It is memories that tattoo tender skin,
pain that holds and pierces, ink etching
indelible pictures refusing to fade with time.

And the crowds admire clear images:
hearts torn; twisted flowers entwined
about innocent crosses; new butterflies
hovering over chaste fleur-de-lis;
snakes coiled, threatening to strike;
scorpions like small crabs in wait to use
the fierce sting; enormous, demonic dragons
dredging flames; finally, the empty skull.

Perhaps you do not see tattoos I wear,
the puckering, wounded flesh, an ache
remaining there for life, pictures hidden
beneath my smile, under sweet songs I sing
and forced, cracked laughter.

MYTH ENDING

At the end of the myth,
Tears mist over the eyes,
Great gulps of wine wash away
A bitter taste
As a new day bandages each wound
With sunshine.

As the myth ends,
sad eyes seem wiser,
fingers letting go of
all the stories told
like flakes scattering
across cold air,
old, old tales sung sadly,
a dirge of the ages.

At last in the myth,
dreams are strewn like seeds
across the greedy earth.
We watch them take hold and
ready themselves to blossom
in new places.

Finally, into the myth,
poets stir words
both sweet and bitter, making
sense of myths ending,
sharing tears, laughter,
and dreams for the future.

TIBETAN MONK

The citrus and red robes
defined a Tibetan monk
but the Ipod in his hand

flew him far away
from Samye, mantras, prayer flags.
His twitching foot signaled

a rap, loud in his ear.
Yet I had to wonder
If he recalled those "one voice

chords" from dreams past.
Did he see quiet yaks
on a slanted, sacred mountain,

the twisting Tsangpo River
lined with Buddha's flock?
This monk hiding a speaker

in his ear, exuded
harmony for all
the universe but his

busy, twitching foot
and bobbing, swaying head
belied a monk's tranquility.

LACE AND POPPIES

Spring, and the jet stream tats lace
for the old mountain. In the valley,
people notice and shake heads sadly,
murmur "Snow again," then recall
seeds beneath the white that will become
glorious fields of poppies splashing bright paint
across the worn land. The mountain shoulders
its lace shawl sweetly, like an old woman,
dreaming, perhaps, of love and youth and flowers
as clouds build winter castles looming high.
Children sniff the air like puppies, smelling
spring and seeing poppies in their dreams.

WORDS FOR A FRIEND

I have nothing to give you, my friend,
but words.
They are yours,
sweet and sour,
hard and soft,
spicy and bland.
Take them and use them
for they grew in my heart.

When I am gone,
my words will linger on yellowed pages
and in your tattered memories.
You will savor their crunch like popcorn,
rolling each buttery sound over your tongue,
tasting the salt of my tears,
the sweet caramel of my love.

They may lie dormant like bulbs of tulips
to bloom in profusion each spring
or trill like bird songs in your apple tree.

MOURNING CARL SANDBURG

In the heart of America
A voice is silent,
Resting in a cool tomb.
And mutely the painted women still
Beckon to a farm boy
And soundlessly the hogs scream
On the butcher's block
And wordless workers walk a picket line
In Chicago.
Back and forth,
Back and forth.

Night comes like fog on black cat's feet . . .
Stalking the flatlands.
Sleeping in silent meadows,
Stretching across the prairie.

But listen—
From beyond the empty shadows
Comes a sound to break your heart . . .
The corn silk fairies are weeping.

IMAGINE THE HARVEST

She harvested words,
finding some discarded among trash,
others within sweet petals of lilies.
Wherever she went, she gleaned words,
noted each carefully and hoarded it
as one stores treasures.

She began each day
clipping words from a sunrise.
Then, as evening slipped in,
she chipped magenta metaphors from sunsets,
and stirred them a bit for color.

She turned her face for rainy words,
reached for a rainbow and tucked it
within her rich store of glories.

She ignored Bach, preferring Vivaldi,
whose images spoke to her need
for mellow melody rendered with dignity.

But she harvested most from Tchaikovsky,
feet twitching, dance born
along with poems, rich with promise,
thick with years of mystery.

Even in her sleep she harvested,
dreaming mystical, whimsical,
cryptic, enigmatic word pictures
she gathered quietly on awakening.

Then at the end of her life,
she gave away all her words,
her legacy to a world too rigid
to read poetry, too busy
to harvest thoughts, too literal
to grasp imagination and hold it
in the palm of one's hand.

DARKNESS HOVERING

When the long darkness hovers
when stars are covered, one by one

and music meanders beneath a black
blanket, soundless, without a song,

I am left to lie still and watch pictures
pulse on my eyelids as I live in memory.

There is nothing so gloomy as this inky
time when musings of you pulse.

I lie still, listening for your kind voice,
the richness of your laughter, the gusto

of your passion, breathless in the sooty,
overpowering blackness of gloom and

hope for sleep to take me to a place
where golden light looms long and lovely.

HAIKUS

Fear

Cold snowball of fear
Ever rolling fast downhill
Gathers icy fright.

Night

Moonbeams cling to trees,
Hanging on with golden hands
Lest they disappear.

Stars

Stars are frozen tears
Of grief for all the lost loves
Whose hot flames turned cold.

Tears

Clustered crystal tears
Creeping down my daughter's cheeks
Flashing bright rainbows

IN THE WILDERNESS

In the wilderness He walked
forty days and nights
learning thirst only as a man
who longs for a drop of water
on his tongue,
devastated by hunger while
dreaming of loaves and fishes,
pierced by loneliness,
harsh as a cold, dark tomb.

In the wilderness He wandered
beneath scattered, shattered stars by night
and scorching, searing sun by day,
remembering the power
of parting the Red Sea,
of draping rainbows across the sky
and looking forward to
walking on water.

In the wilderness He wrestled
With a fallen angel
Using words like swords,
like seven trumpets of ram's horns
leaving behind rocks like loaves of bread
oozing sorrow for the Son of God.

JAZZ IN THE LOUNGE

Here is shredded jazz amongst blue smoke,
hanging in the air in pieces, like petals
blowing in the wind, crowd catching

a few, along with the syncopated
beat bouncing across the bar. The band
grooves on and on as martinis are shaken,

margaritas salted, beers passed.
Little flakes of jazz fall like snow,
each segment hitting the ears, the heart,

the soul. The crowd gasps, leaning in
to catch the next shred of music before it
melts away into oblivion.

This is like chasing butterflies.
Music flitting about the room, bobbing
here and there cannot be pinned down.

The thread of melody is lost but the beat
holds us like a moth to a flame.
Here is a new sort of poetry

without words, harsh sounds blending
with soft notes born on the Mississippi.
The band wears each gaudy strain with ease.

Listeners suck in the sounds along
with their drinks, tasting specks of jazz
and finding each one spicy on the palate.

LIFE

No one ever told me life
is a ride on a train
rolling quick as laughter through joy,
but scheduled slow through pain.

No one ever said the children
whose hands I held tightly
would so swiftly slip away to
run pell-mell through the aisles
until they found their own car.

No one dared speak
about desolate station stops
and leave-taking without good-byes,
of cries for those who left
while strangers boarded
with murder in their eyes.

No one had courage
to warn that at the end
my car would be so empty
and my wrinkled hand
would clutch a ticket
I can't remember how to read.

AT THE END

At the end, she wakened
drenched in blood and tears.
Those twins, Pain and Sorrow,

stalked her dreams by night,
her every thought by day.
At the end, they leapt

from the cabled bridge
between light and dark,
between joy and grief

between past and future
until the shattered, scattered
love she once felt

became an ugly, shadowed
photo with tattered corners.
Years later, she

was the only one
who could see the blood
and tears across the print.

FIRE AND MIST

My days are of fire and mist, mist and fire.
Dreams drift in, blue over these green hills
as wisps of wanton wishes wait in trees.
Day barely breaks in mauve murmurings.
I turn from ashes of the night and walk
into day, tilting my face, flower-like,
for dewdrops or salty tears gathering there.

My days are of fire and mist, mist and fire.
Flames and shadows dance in a ring at my feet.
and I am only half warm, with mists across
my shoulders like a cold, damp cloak.
Silver smoke slips over these dark hills
to hide a sometimes moon and I am held,
moth-like, to a flame I dare not touch
until I am a shadow or a mist.

ECHOCARDIOGRAM

Someone is eavesdropping on my heart.
Wires taped to my chest
reveal ocean sounds swishing
rhythmically and without ceasing.
I am not sure whether my tide is in or out,
but I lie here listening to my own
private heart swooshes,
remembering to breathe,
trying to pray.

This is new territory.
Once I took for granted
my heart would always beat.

Once I paid no attention
when an occasional flutter
like a swarm of moths
paused in my chest for a brief rest.

Now I know there is this ocean sound
and I am the beach,
longing for the waves to last forever.

HIS CAVE

The cave held poems born
from dark places of the heart.
Products of pain, they clung to each page
clawing their way to notoriety,
each unique, each spoken
as God speaks, with authority.

The cave held the poet captive
by the light of day and through
purple nights heavy with promise.
Delighting only in his words
or himself, he passed the time
stanza by stanza, not noticing
his soul withering or his spirit shrinking.

Once, long ago, the poet
marked his life lightly with laughter
relishing a sun announcing
morning in the eastern sky
and evening with blushes at twilight.
The times he dared to love and sing
and hope grew shorter as the darkness
squeezed his life tighter and tighter.

Now words like tears scatter across
his pages as he ages quickly.
His cave becomes his only safe place
where Plato's shadows crowd reality.

His poems are finely polished perceptions
of all the things he cannot see
except with his mind's eye
and his fiercely pounding heart.

The world awaits his next poem,
stunned perhaps, that something so bright
could come from so dark a place,
a little like a lone star
penned to a black sky
shining shining shining shining.

LISTEN

Listen.
The children are speaking
And truth rolls like marbles from their lips.
Listen well, for the jump rope turns quickly
And the years of listening are gone.

Listen.
The children are crying.
While you lie in your bed of unlistening,
The doll is broken,
The game is lost,
And you are the loser.

MAGICIAN

My grandfather was a magician.
His first disappearing trick came soon after
he planted his seed in my grandmother's womb.

My father popped out nine months later like
a rabbit out of a hat, unaware
his wayward father sawed women in half

under an old circus tent across the rural south.
My grandfather caused audiences to moan in fright
from ghosts he stirred by his magic.

Children echoed his "Abracadabra"
when he pulled coins from their ears.
(His magic never worked on scarred hearts.)

MEMORY OF YOU

No one knows the way
you come and go upon my heart
like the silent tug of tide.

No one feels the fog of you
feathering reality.
I am like an island
lost in the misty distance.

You are the harsh taste of salt,
the bitterness of tears
upon a cold, wet winter beach.

Your name has not been said aloud in years,
yet it clings like coral to the roof of my mouth,
cutting, cutting.

I have become a large pink conch
washed up on the sand
and loud with the memory of you.

MEMORIES ARE ONLY

Memories are only
Tattoos on the brain,
Pain-etched, day by day,
Brush-stroked in joy.
Then when we are asleep
The pictures come alive
To waken us with tears.

MOOD INDIGO

In the smoky quiet of a day nearly gone,
I sip amber champagne and dream purple jazz.
The day's glacial tension slides off my body,
melting at my feet, indigo tears.
Silvery fluttering wings brush my cheeks.

I will spend my evening savoring
Sweet-memoried golden ambrosia
and reading Kahlil Gibran until my soul
swings lightly in a hammock. I will sleep
to the soothing sound of lavender bells
pealing across an innocent night.

OF DARKNESS GOING

The day came in and
quietly sculpted shapes from darkness.
It laid its head across the valley,
blood-staining bony tree tops,
spilling over heaps of shadowed leaves.

The cool blue of night stood in pools,
turning purple from spattered drops of sun-red.
The earth, reluctant to surrender night,
bled.

And I knew,
as my world hung suspended between day and night,
What God must have seen when He said,
"Let there be light."

OREGON BEACH TOWN IN MARCH

This town wears its salt air
like a tattered old sweater,
weathers storms and sun alike.
At this age it accepts whatever comes
year after year, face a bit wrinkled
but hunkered down in comfort.

It sits silently within
sea sand and salt,
tsunami sirens in readiness,
silent sentries on call while
white-edged waves move peacefully
from far out across the Pacific.

Fierce squalls visit briefly,
salty rain pitting windows,
pelting sand, wind whistling
around corners, across singing shingles,
down the tilted, tired chimneys.

But when the sky and sea
regain their youthful blue,
when the sand holds spring's warmth
even for a few hours,
people storm the beach
with ecstatic dogs, giddy children,
galloping kites, runners pounding
alongside the drumming surf.

Waves glide in on the shine,
chrome bumpers glittering in the sun.
Gulls call out to one another.
Folks drag out the ladders and paint
to doll up the old town
just in time for another summer of fun.

MOTHER'S CLOSET

In the cluttered closets of my mind,
I sort through Mother's clothing.
Her perfume clings
to each abandoned garment
as though she were out
for a short drive
and would return.

She has been gone for years,
her clothing distributed
to someone glad to wear a size eight
smelling of White Shoulders.
But each night,
I rummage in her closet,
making indecent heaps
of her cherished things.

Smothered by her scent,
I feel somehow afraid
she has returned and will
find nothing to wear.

RESURRECTION

After black nights stretching
like a tunnel through winter,
after a dark mask
clapped over my face,
the smothering stygian
blanket of midnight,
lasting lasting lasting,

after the thin red ridge
of momentary daylight,
flashes of Northern Lights
falling from a frozen sky,
a full-bodied wine of twilight
dulling the senses,

after days of bright white
bouncing peak to peak,
plastering a cold earth
with blinding light
blanching shadows,
luminous
with absence of color,

after the winter-long
lack of hues,
comes bursting through
the thin cap of snow,
comes rising
like a hope of life,
comes springing up
victorious,
a slim, tender, tendril,
a fresh, virulent,
verdant shoot of green.

Allelujah!

PRAISING TOMORROW

I will not choose to walk the well-worn path
Where once the tender violets have bled
And weeping rainbows withered overhead.

I shall not smell red roses from past years
Or hear the same sad songs, repeat the dance.
I will not turn around for one last glance.

This then, my friend, please try to understand.
Old paths are overgrown, tangled and tried.
Tired tears are cried; at last my eyes are dried.

I take the road uncharted, heading out
To seek a place untouched and pure and bright
And gather stars and moonbeams in each night.

I do not waver in my lonely trek,
Exploring each frontier with new-found zest,
Panning each shiny grain of gold to test.

This is my pledge. I will not look back,
Not even once, to taste the bitter sorrow.
For now I wait with hope each glad tomorrow.

SENIOR SWIMMERS

They gather here like ancient elephants
hovering at the watering hole.
And in the immaculate water
they pretend they are young.

Men flaunt Atlas abs they once owned.
Women spill out of swimsuits,
with used body parts that titillated
so many years ago. They dream
of mirrors reflecting skin like a peach,
firm, juicy days when a swimsuit
was a simple route to the erotic.

Music skims across the blue pool,
haunting as a lover's moon, and
as one they sway and reminisce.
The redhead struts a leathery body
adorned in yellow polka dot, body taut
and tight. The old guys gape,
dreaming about what they once dared
as ancient hormones flare for a moment.

The air is full of conversation . . .
grandchildren, doctors, throes of living
and, in hushed voices, who just died.
Even laughter here comes frosted with misery,
and smiles don't always shine with joy
as the water baptizes them for a new "golden age"
alive with memory, yet scarred by reality.

TIDAL SPIRIT

The ghost of the sea sweeps in on the tide,
breathing a dampness from out of a tomb,
writing white hieroglyphs on darkened sand,
droning a dirge for a cold, vacant shell.

The ghost of the sea sweeps in on the tide
riding warm wind to the hot desert surf,
rippling sand billows with sulphurous breath,
sniffing out fossils forgotten one day.

The ghost of the sea sweeps in on the tide,
plotting emotions by ebb and by flow,
waging of wars and the planting of seeds,
laughing at man dominated by moon.

SOUNDS OF SAIGON IN SEATTLE

Sounds of Saigon sing across
the manicure shop in melodious voices
as nails are painted artistically.
Customers do not understand a single word,
mesmerized as they are
by sounds from far across the Pacific.

Although the girls wear western dress,
something about the scene makes one
think of crisp white ao dais
like lotus blossoms in the canals of Saigon.

They call to one another playfully as though
from a brightly painted dragon boat.
The workplace is festive with happy chattering
exported mysteriously to the western world.

It is much like an operetta sung in some sort
of far Eastern rhythm and harmony.
Nails buffed, polished, with the sounds of Saigon
slipping across the room like
sanpans across the Mekong Delta.
The audience will not applaud
for fear of ruining their fingernails.

YOUNG WIDOW

She wakes her children with a smile and kiss
Plugs in the coffee pot—begins her day
With childish chatter, snips of that and this,
The standard tasks performed the standard way.
With children off to school, she stops awhile
To visit with a friend. She talks too fast
And laughs too loudly; then with pasted smile
She takes her leave. A day can only last
At most from now to now, from sun to sun,
From mask to mask. But every word unsaid
Is conversation with the dead. And one
Must show control. Be normal. Put to bed
Each child. And then away from prying eyes,
She climbs into her empty bed and cries.

TURTLE WALK

Darkness finds its way tonight only to tight spaces
a round white turtle moon cannot reach.
The sea holds flashes of light like tiny silver eggs,
scattering them across the waiting sand.

People line the shore expectantly,
eyes scanning a dark horizon.
The wait seems long and hopeless.
Impatience takes the crowd as
a silent sea keeps its secrets
beneath a pregnant moon.

Finally she comes,
scrawling ageless tracks across the sand,
following a primordial command.
She moves with slow purpose,
ending her slow trek above the tide line.
The trance begins.
A patient moon swims the midnight sky.

At last her work is done,
The dream complete.
Her journey ends with tracks
back to a quiet sea.
The sand is empty once again,
save for this mound full of promises.

LOVING WORDS

I am in love with words.
I collect them,
Sniff them out,
Snag them from the wind,
Pluck them
From innocent mouths of children,
Cram my pockets
Full of stolen words
Sweet as candies
To suck later
When my mouth is dry.

SONG OF THE PUB DOG

On the Isle of Mull in the old stone pub
There's ale in the jug and fire on the hearth.
A little white Scottie lies at their feet
And all is well, Lads, all is well.

The stories told o'er their foamy pints,
With hot tears shed for all who've gone,
Brings solace from the wee white dog
And all is well, Lads, all is well.

A fiddle plays its mournful tunes
As ghosts settle down on the empty stools
And hands reach for the comforting dog
All is well, Lads, all is well.

Songs are sung as the pints are drained
Laced with old stories of that place
One man holds the pub dog on his lap
Then all is well, Lads, all is well.

The evening wanes, the fire goes cold
Feeling soused, they take their leave
And the little dog gets one last pat
Knowing all is well, Lads, all is well.

SCULPTOR

Life is a sculptor,
shaping us as we go,
chiseling memories

we choose to lose,
chunks of stone scattered
on the floor of our past.

We either remain
on a pedestal,
arms raised in victory,

eyes seeing the future,
shoulders fairly squared
against the elements,

or we crumble under
the sculptor's deft pressure,
falling at last to the ground.

Dust returns to dust,
all promise failed,
then art curtailed.

LULLABIES

It is night and houses hold
a hallowed hour of simple sweetness,
subtle glow at the core,
comfort framed within each window.

Inside, mothers invent lullabies
to hush their babies with lilting notes
neatly swathed in small blankets,
tenderly sung from rocking chairs.

Comforting songs stream across darkness
showing the way to infant dreams.
Innocent faces smile as though
angels whispered their mothers' voice.

There is a certain tranquility
within the refuge of these walls,
a torch passed grandmother to mother,
gifts of lyrics for each child

generations of selfless love
meted out in melody,
magic music meant to soothe
timeless singing across the years.

ONLY IN STILLNESS

Only between heartbeats
and wave beats,

only as a quiet fog
settles like gray grief,

only between wails
of a foghorn

as silent ships
turn back like ghosts,

only in stillness
can knowledge come

like a deep-drawn breath
of spirit and truth,

using eyes blinded
with the sting

of salt spray
turned inward

to see one's self.

POEMS STIRRED

I have grown old, my love.
Words I stored like sliced apples
to dry on the roof
are waiting to be folded
into a tangy autumn pie
or stirred into a smooth sauce
sweetened with the savor of my life.

I have grown old, my love.
My arthritic fingers write slowly
barely keeping up with wrinkled thoughts
from the cloth of a lifetime.

Stories I heard as a child,
songs sung as I fought sleep,
sayings that salted my grandmother's speech,
laughter, tears, rage and acquiescence
simmered through years
into the slow syrup of these days.

My poems will be spiced and stirred until
the essence is exactly right.
I will give you the first taste.

WALKING A NEW TRAIL

I do not know this place,
Yet memories stir silent shadows.
Sunlight presses golden droplets
In an old familiar way.

I do not know this space,
Yet just around the bend, somehow I know
A laurel blooms like lace, and way up high
A tall birch wears a heart with two names.

These woods have never seen my face
And yet my spirit skips along this trail
As one returning home from a long journey
Enjoying landmarks from the past.

THINGS THAT MAKE ME CRY

The soft percussive sound of your wings
beating on high as they head into
the blue infinity of sky . . .

Fizzy jazz shaken into my martini
along with the green olive
at the end of a used-up day . . .

Fire fading across the hearth,
my heart tick-ticking in slow time
with the flickering flames . . .

Old photos where the past lives on,
and youth stays in its glossy place
beside laughter and love . . .

Your soft breathing as you sleep
deep beneath your dreams,
while stars light your way across the night.

BIRTHDAY MOON

On her birthday,
she watched a fragile moon
float bravely, brazenly
on a wrinkled sea.
It rose in aching stillness,
spine bent awkwardly,
yet light dazzling the waters
as in times past.

It hovered, as though to plunge
back in for a lonely swim,
lurched to begin its climb
up the smooth sky trail
among stepping stone stars.
Paling in the strain
like a white-haired old woman,
it traveled the worn night path.

CLASSICAL GUITAR

Memories of other centuries
live within this instrument,
slipping along twisting streets
within ancient walls.

This music serves up bowls
of colorful paella
cooked fresh from the sea,
memories of making love
beside a fiery bougainvillea,
sounds of quick feet stomping
a hot blooded, racy flamenco.

Yet there is gentleness here,
quiet tones smoothing stress,
tunes playing on the mind,
dreams of old love and new.
It sings of a mysterious,
elegant simplicity . . .

A candle glowing in the dark,
praying in a Romanesque church,
two lovers sharing red wine
and the soft sounds of a Latin language
sung in mellifluous music of long ago.

OLD MAN

He wears twilight about bent shoulders
like a much blessed prayer shawl.
His eyes hold fast to his past,
not grasping the hidden future.

He shows a guileless smile of a child
As he tosses laughter like a beach ball
bouncing on the wrinkled surf
of fragile memory.

No talk of aging is allowed,
no laments or downcast eyes.
He fingers moments like a rosary,
his final comfort, a prayer for submission.

HONEYED LIGHT OF AUTUMN

It is autumn, and the honeyed light
flows across trees sticky with color.
This is Vivaldi's stash of leaves
flung across a stiff staff of notes.

A moon hangs swollen and burning
in a pompous purple sky filled with
sweet and tangy songs tasting of cider.
Star chips scatter, then melt like summer gone.

This is the time for breathing in slowly
and feeling autumn enter the blood
like a heady flask of whiskey warming you,
prolonging the eventual entrance of Winter.

POSSIBILITY

The possibility of sweet red wine
within each pitcher of clear water,
the improbable promise of an empty tomb,
the conjecture of walking on water,
calming seas, feeding a multitude
with only a few loaves and fishes
is the holding power that brings me
to my knees, head bowed, lips moving
in prayers full of powerful potential
for miracles, for wonder, for praise.